The Wisdom of the Crows

AND OTHER BUDDHIST TALES

Retold by
Sherab Chödzin & Alexandra Kohn

Illustrated by
Marie Cameron

TRICYCLE PRESS
Berkeley, California

CONTENTS

FOREWORD

Buddhism has its origins in the life and teachings of the Buddha, formerly Prince Siddhartha. His father, who reigned in northern India during the sixth century BC, was king of the powerful Sakya tribe. As a young man, Siddhartha escaped from his father's palace by stealth and set forth on a search for the true meaning and purpose of life. After many years of meditation accompanied by extreme practices such as prolonged fasting, Siddhartha abandoned the tortures of asceticism for the middle way, a balance between all extremes. His meditation then bore fruit. In Bodh Gaya, now the modern Indian state of Bihar, Siddhartha attained enlightenment sitting in meditation beneath the Bodhi Tree. Thus he became the Buddha, "the awakened one."

Seven weeks after his enlightenment, the Buddha began to teach others, forming a community of monks and nuns. Their teachings soon spread beyond India: south to Sri Lanka, Burma, Thailand, Laos, Cambodia and Indonesia; north to China, Vietnam, Korea, Japan, Mongolia, Russia, Tibet, Bhutan and Nepal. For many centuries, Buddhism flourished in these Asian countries, though the twentieth century has seen a decline in some places. Since the Second World War, however, Buddhism has found a new home in the West, and it is currently the fastest-growing religion in Europe and the USA.

The tales in this collection, which are taken from several Asian cultures, illustrate various aspects of Buddhist thought. Since Buddhism is a non-theistic religion, its expression is to a great extent simply basic human wisdom. Though traditional tales from Buddhist cultures are often alive with gods, goddesses, and lesser spirits and ghosts, these are not regarded as independent entities but rather in essence as virtues and powers of mind. In the Chinese tale "The Living Kuan Yin," the hero's generosity and kindness naturally lead him to connect with a deeper level of compassion in himself (personified by the goddess Kuan Yin), which truly has the power to answer questions and grant wishes. The theme of self-sacrificing generosity leading to the acquisition of a feminine power recurs in "Goodheart and the Goddess of the Forest," which comes from Myanmar (formerly Burma). In this story, ensuing developments show how the ego is threatened by the supernormal abilities goodness has gained, and seeks to regain its control. The shoe is on the other foot in "The Conch Maiden," a Tibetan tale, where the initial virtue

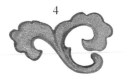

takes a feminine form and finds fruition in a semi-divine male principle. Conch is pure white, yet flashes with all the colors. In contrast with gold and silver, it represents a wealth that is more than just the riches of this world: the wealth that lies in the true nature of mind itself.

One of the fundamental Buddhist values is humor, which views life as real but also somewhat transparent. Hardly a better example of Buddhist humor in the Tibetan mold can be found than in "The Foolish Boy." Meditators young and old will readily recognize the boy's romping, guileless gullibility as a representation of the lively movements of our own thought patterns. Happily the boy has a kind of natural sweetness, which attracts capable caretakers like his mother and wife. We also see here how simple-mindedness sometimes comes close to genius, for both break the rule of concept.

The genius of no-concept is also evoked in "The Wisdom of the Crows," where we learn that once awareness is allowed to settle into a concept, it becomes fixed and predictable, and is easily defeated. This is one of Buddhism's key insights, one which lies at the center of training in Buddhist meditation and the martial arts.

Humor also comes to the fore in others of the short Zen tales that have been included. In stories like "Useless Work" or "Where Are You Going?" we find the art of the punchline that packs a mind-lifting zap. "The Stone Ape," a longer tale from China, is a light-hearted story that also has a shocking punchline, but in this case it involves a sobering leap of perspective, in which we see that no matter how far we go, our mind always goes along with us.

"The Man Who Didn't Want to Die," from Japan, is an engaging and provocative dance illustrating two typically Buddhist concerns—the capricious nature of desire and the ego's fear of death. Finally the Indian tale "Angulimala the Brigand," in which the hero becomes a holy man, is one of the best-known canonical stories of the Buddha's life.

These stories reflect many profound truths of the Buddha's teaching, but no matter how profound, the truth is always simple and can usually be grasped by young children at least as easily as adults. Life "as the Buddha taught" is like a dream; we must not trifle with it, but we must not take it too seriously either. In these stories, there is always a certain lightness, changeability and play that makes it easy for fundamental warmth, intelligence and humor to come shining through.

THE LIVING KUAN YIN

Once, long ago, in China there was a young man named Chin Po-wan. His name fitted him well, because Chin means "gold" and Po-wan means "million," and Po-wan's family had more golden coins than they could count.

Because of his name and family fortune, Po-wan thought he would always be rich, so he spent his money very freely—but not on himself. Feeling truly sorry for the poor and needy, he could never refuse them help. A poor man had only to hold out his hand and Po-wan filled it with gold. If he heard of a widow with hungry children, he made sure that they had a place to live and food for the rest of their lives. Po-wan gave unselfishly to all who were poor and without hope.

But finally, even Po-wan's huge fortune was not enough. He gave away so much that he became a poor man himself. When at last he himself had only a little food, he continued to give food to those with even less. One day, as he was sharing his bowl of rice with a beggar, he suddenly felt very sad that he had so little to give.

"Why am I so poor?" he asked himself. "I have never done anything to harm anyone, and I have never spent much money on myself. How can it be that I don't have more to give this poor man than a handful of rice?"

This question preoccupied him for days and nights, and still no answer came to him. Then at last he had an idea. He would go to see the living Kuan Yin, the beautiful goddess of mercy and kindness to whom all people looked for comfort, especially those who were in trouble. "Kuan Yin knows both the past and the future," he thought. "Surely she can answer my question."

So Chin Po-wan set out for the South Sea where Kuan Yin lived. He traveled through many strange lands, until one day he came to a broad, rushing river. He was standing on the bank wondering how he could possibly get across, when he heard a deep, rumbling voice coming from the cliff above him.

"Chin Po-wan," the voice said, "if you are going to the South Sea, would you ask the living goddess Kuan Yin a question for me?"

Po-wan had never refused anything to anybody in his whole life. Besides, he knew the goddess allowed each person who came to her three questions, and he only had one of his own. So he replied, "Yes, yes; all right, I will."

Turning around, he looked up to see who the voice had come from. To his amazement, towering above him he saw a huge snake, whose body was as thick as a temple pillar and twice as long. Po-wan was frightened, and he was glad that he had been quick to agree.

"Then please ask her why I am not yet a dragon, even though I have practiced kindness and self-control for a thousand years," said the big snake.

"Oh, I surely will!" said Po-wan nervously, hoping that the big reptile would continue to practice kindness and self-control and not eat him up in one gulp. "That is, if I can get across this river. I'll never see Kuan Yin unless I can reach the other side, and at the moment I don't see how I can do it."

"Oh, that's no problem," said the snake. "Just jump on my back and I'll carry you across."

So Po-wan climbed on to the snake's broad scaly back and was soon safely across the river. He thanked the huge creature politely and said goodbye. Then he continued on his way towards the South Sea.

He walked a lot further that day and was getting quite hungry when, luckily, he came to an inn where he was able to buy a bowl of rice. While waiting for his food, he had a chat with the innkeeper. He told him about the great snake who had taken him across the river and learned that the creature was well known to the people of the region. He was called the Serpent of the Cliff and was well liked because he kept bandits and other evil-doers from crossing the river. As Po-wan was telling the innkeeper about his adventure, it came out that he was on his way to see the living Kuan Yin.

"Oh," said the innkeeper. "I would be so grateful if you would ask her a question for me. I have a daughter who is beautiful, good-hearted and clever. Yet she is now twenty years old and has never uttered a single word in her whole life. Could you please, please ask the goddess why she cannot talk?"

Po-wan could hardly refuse a request like this, so he told the innkeeper, "Don't worry about a thing. I'll ask about your daughter for you, and I'm sure everything will turn out to be all right for her." After all, Po-wan thought to himself, I am allowed three questions and I only need to ask one for myself.

Po-wan continued on his journey, and by nightfall, he was hungry again and tired. There was no inn to be found, so he knocked on the door of the largest

house he could find and asked to stay the night. The wealthy owner of the house welcomed him, gave him a good meal and something to drink, and then showed him to a lovely guest room. Po-wan woke up the next morning refreshed and ready to go. He thanked his host and said goodbye.

"Where will your journey take you?" his host asked.

"Oh, I am going to the South Sea," replied Po-wan.

"Well, if you are going to the South Sea, perhaps you will see the living Kuan Yin and could ask her a question for me. I have been living in this house for twenty years and all that time I have taken the very best care of my garden. Yet no plant has ever borne flowers or fruit, which is bad enough; but what's more, because of that, the birds never come to my garden and sing, and there is no nectar for the bees to gather. My garden is such a sad place. I would be grateful if you could ask the goddess why this is so."

"I would be honored to ask her your question," said Po-wan and continued on his way. He did want to help the kind man with his garden, and besides, the living Kuan Yin allowed each person three questions, and he only had one of his own, one for the snake, one for the innkeeper and one for the man with the garden. "Uh-oh…" Po-wan thought. He stopped and counted the questions on his fingers. Yes, he realized with a flutter of his heart, there was definitely one question too many.

What a predicament! He had four important questions to ask. One of them would have to go unanswered, but which one should it be? If he didn't ask his own question, his whole journey would be for nothing. But if he didn't ask the snake's question, or the innkeeper's, or the question of the man who had so kindly lodged and fed him, not only would one of them be very disappointed, but he would also be breaking a promise. As Po-wan walked, he turned the problem over and over in his mind.

Finally, he thought to himself, "I made the promises, therefore I must keep them. Besides, even if I don't ask my own question, my journey won't be for nothing. At least those three people will have their problems solved."

Happy with this decision, Po-wan came to the South Sea. He asked local people for directions and at last came into the presence of the living Kuan Yin. The goddess was so beautiful and radiated such kindness that Po-wan felt very meek and humble. He bowed to her and then quietly asked her his questions.

"The Serpent of the Cliff," he began, "has been practicing kindness and self-control for a thousand years, but he has not yet become a dragon. Why is this?"

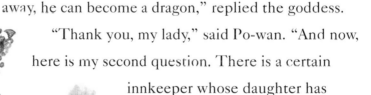

"On the serpent's head there are seven shining pearls. If six of them are taken away, he can become a dragon," replied the goddess.

"Thank you, my lady," said Po-wan. "And now, here is my second question. There is a certain innkeeper whose daughter has reached the age of twenty without uttering a single word. Why should this be?"

"Because of things that happened in her past lives, it is her destiny

11

to be unable to speak until she sets her eyes on the man who is to be her husband."

"Thank you again, my lady," said Po-wan. "And now for my last question: there is a rich man who welcomed me into his house. He has a garden that he has tended well for many years, but no plant or tree there has ever flowered or borne fruit. What is the reason for that?"

"There are seven jars of gold and silver buried in his garden," replied the living Kuan Yin. "If he gives away half of that wealth, his garden will bloom and bear fruit."

Po-wan respectfully thanked Kuan Yin a final time. As he bowed and backed away, she gave him the most wonderful smile, which filled his heart with joy. Then Po-wan sat under a tree and wrote down what she had told him, so he would be sure not to forget a word. Then he began his journey home.

First he stopped at the rich man's house and recounted what the goddess had told him about the gold and silver in his garden. The rich man was so grateful to know how his garden could become beautiful at last that he gave Po-wan half his treasure.

Next Po-wan came to the town where the inn was. The innkeeper's daughter saw him from the window and immediately called out, "Oh, Chin Po-wan, you've come back from the South Sea. What did the kind goddess say?"

The innkeeper was filled with happiness at hearing his daughter speaking at last. The two young people had fallen in love at first sight, and the innkeeper insisted that they be married.

Then Po-wan went to the rushing river to give the snake the living Kuan Yin's message. The snake removed six of the pearls and gave them to Po-wan. Immediately he turned into a magnificent dragon, and the one remaining pearl in his forehead began to give out a powerful glow, which filled the countryside with a soft, gorgeous light.

That is how Chin Po-wan, through his kindness and generosity, married a beautiful wife and once again became as rich as his name.

13

THE MOST IMPORTANT THING

Once a famous Chinese poet wanted to study the wisdom of the Buddha. He traveled a long distance to see a famous teacher and asked him, "What is the most important thing in the Buddha's teaching?"

"Don't harm anyone and only do good," replied the teacher.

"This is just too stupid!" exclaimed the poet. "You are supposed to be a great teacher, so I traveled miles and miles to see you. And now is that all you can come up with? Even a three-year-old could say that!"

"Maybe a three-year-old could say it, but it is very hard to put into practice, even for a very old man like myself," said the teacher.

THE MAN WHO DIDN'T WANT TO DIE

Long, long ago, in Japan, there lived a man named Sentaro. He had inherited money from his father and had enough to live on, so he never worked. He just loafed through life until he was thirty-two years old. Then, one day, for no particular reason, he started thinking about sickness and death. He knew that everybody had to become sick and die some time, but he had never thought about it. Now he couldn't get rid of the idea that this was going to happen to him, and he started to feel very, very bad.

"People's lives are so short," he thought. "I would like to live at least five or six hundred years without getting ill." And he began to wonder how he could actually do this.

Sentaro had heard the story of a Chinese emperor who had also wanted to escape death. The emperor was rich and powerful and could do whatever he

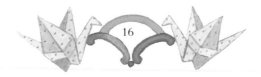

wanted, but, like everyone else, he still had to die. He felt sad about this, just as Sentaro did, and he wished for the same thing: to be able to live for a long, long time, or maybe even forever. This great emperor sent one of his trusted counselors, a man named Jofoku, who until then had been able to accomplish anything he was told to accomplish, to find something called the elixir of life. According to stories they had heard, if you drank the elixir of life, you would live forever.

Jofoku set off across the sea to find the elixir of life, in a boat loaded with jewels and gold to pay for it. But he never returned. Sadly, without the elixir of life, the great emperor had to die just like everybody else.

But the story about Jofoku and the elixir of life lived on. According to what people told Sentaro now, Jofoku had gone to heaven and become a god, and the god Jofoku had become the special protector of hermits. Hermits were people who lived alone in the high mountains and spent their time meditating. People said that the hermits knew the secret of the elixir of life, and if Sentaro wanted to find it, he would have to ask them.

So Sentaro set off to get the elixir of life from the hermits. He wandered through all the high mountains of Japan, but he never found a single hermit. Bandits he found, in their hide-outs in the mountains, but this didn't help him.

After he had spent a long time walking and climbing by himself in the mountains without success, he became very discouraged. But he didn't give up,

because he was still troubled by
the idea that he was going to have to die.

Finally, one day he heard about a temple to Jofoku, where you
could worship this god of the hermits who had once set out to find the elixir of
life. Sentaro found this temple, which was in a lonely spot in a mountain forest.
He went inside and began to pray. He prayed for seven days, begging Jofoku to
help him find a hermit who could fulfill his wish. At midnight on the seventh day,
a door on the little cabinet on top of the altar flew open, and Jofoku came out.
Hovering near Sentaro in the midst of a shining cloud, he spoke to him.

"To find the elixir of life, you would have to become a hermit yourself. A
hermit's life is too hard for you. A hermit has to eat only berries and the bark of
trees. He has to stay alone until his heart becomes as pure as gold and free from
all desires. Finally, after a long time, the hermit feels neither hunger nor heat nor
cold. His body becomes so light he can walk on water or ride on a bird. But you
have been an idle man, used to comfort. You could never do this. So I will answer
your prayer in another way. I will send you to the Land of Neverending Life,
where no one ever dies."

With this, Jofoku put a tiny little crane, made of folded paper, into Sentaro's
hand and told him to sit on its back. At once, the crane began to grow, and soon it
was large enough for Sentaro to sit on it quite comfortably. It spread its wings and
rose high into the air. Together they soared over the mountains and out across the

ocean. For many days they flew over the waves, until at last they reached an island. The crane landed in the middle of the island, and as soon as Sentaro got off its back, it folded itself up and went into his pocket.

Sentaro was very curious about this Land of Neverending Life. He walked around the country and then into the nearby town to talk to the people who lived there. Of course everything was very strange and very different from his own country. But the people seemed prosperous enough and there was plenty to eat, so he decided he should stay there.

At first he stayed at an inn. But when he told the innkeeper that he had come to the island for good, the innkeeper kindly found him a house and helped him to make all the arrangements necessary to stay there. So the Land of Neverending Life became Sentaro's new home. He even set up a business for himself.

As time went on, Sentaro found out more about his island. The strangest thing of all, of course, was that no one could remember anyone ever dying or even getting ill. This made Sentaro very happy. He was very much looking forward to living forever, and he thought that the islanders must be the happiest people on earth. But this was not true at all. The people grew very bored and tired of their long, long, neverending lives. Things were the same, day after day, year after year. They wished very much to die, for it would be such an interesting change. On top

20

of this, they had heard of a heaven or paradise, which you could enter only by dying. This sounded like something different and wonderful, and they were willing to try anything so they could die and go there. Whenever merchants came from distant lands, the islanders crowded around their booths trying to buy poisons. These they swallowed eagerly, but the poisons only made their health better. The most popular drink on the whole island was a potion that sometimes gave the drinker a few gray hairs and some stomach pains after he had drunk it every day for a hundred years. Poisonous snakes and fish were the islanders' favorite food, but still no one died. People didn't even catch colds.

Sentaro thought these people were strange, but for a long time he was happy in the Land of Neverending Life. His business went well, and he always took pleasure in the idea that he would never die. But after many years, things began to change for Sentaro. He, too, became weary of an endless number of days, always the same. He started to have trouble with his business, and he was always getting into arguments with his neighbors. After about three hundred years, he was very tired and bored, and he began to be homesick. He wanted to get away from the Land of Neverending Life and go to his old country again, where it was possible for people to die.

One day, Sentaro was trying to think of a way to get home, when suddenly he remembered Jofoku. He called out to Jofoku to help him, and as soon as the words were out of his mouth, the paper crane, which had been in the pocket of his old coat all this time, came flying to him and began to grow again to its full size. Sentaro climbed on to its back, and soon they were high in the air, flying over the ocean back towards Japan.

You'd think Sentaro would be happy, but no—not at all! Less than an hour had passed before he began to regret leaving all he had left behind on the island, and especially his neverending life. He tried to turn the crane back, but it took no

notice of him and continued to fly resolutely over the ocean towards Japan.

After a day or two of flying, storm clouds began to form and then rain fell in great sheets. The paper crane got wet, lost its shape and fell into the sea, Sentaro along with him. Sentaro struggled to stay afloat. There was no ship in sight, and he was terribly frightened of drowning. As he looked around for help, what he saw instead was a huge shark coming towards him with a gaping mouth full of sharp teeth. Sentaro tried to cry for help, but he was so terrified that no sound would come from his mouth. When the shark was only a few inches away and he thought his end had come for sure, Sentaro finally managed to get out a huge scream, and he screamed as loud as he could for Jofoku to save him.

Sentaro woke up screaming and found he was on the floor in the lonely Jofoku temple on the mountainside. He had fallen asleep while praying, and all his adventures—the paper crane, the Land of Neverending Life, and the storm and the shark—had been nothing but a dream. A bright light came towards him, and in the light stood a messenger, holding a book.

This is what the messenger told Sentaro:

22

"In answer to your prayers, Jofoku sent you a dream so you could see the Land of Neverending Life. But you grew weary of living there and begged to go back to your own country so you could die. Then Jofoku made you fall into the ocean and sent the shark, so you could die. But you didn't really want to die either, and you cried out for help. Then you woke up here.

"So you see, Sentaro, you don't want to live for ever, and you are in no hurry to die either. So the best thing for you to do is to go back to your home and lead a good life. Be good to your elders and be good to your children, and be a kind and generous friend, and you will find real happiness. Here is a book full of wisdom to show you how to lead the kind of life I have pointed out to you."

Then the messenger disappeared. Taking the book, Sentaro went back to his old home. He studied the book and did his best to follow its wisdom. He gave up his desire to live forever and his desire to die. He gave up his selfishness and did his best to help other people. And he lived in contentment to a ripe old age.

23

USELESS WORK

An old monk and a young monk were walking along the road when they came to a rushing stream. It was neither too wide nor too deep and they were about to wade across when a beautiful young woman, who had been waiting on the bank, approached them. She was elegantly dressed and she fluttered her fan and batted her eyelashes, smiling at them with big eyes.

"Oh," she said, "the current is so swift, the water is so cold, and if my kimono gets wet, it will spoil the silk. Won't one of you please carry me across the stream?" And she edged invitingly towards the young monk.

Now the young monk thought the woman's behavior was disgusting. He thought she was spoiled and shameless and ought to be taught a lesson. On top of that, monks are not supposed to have anything to do with women. So he ignored

her completely and waded across the stream. But the old monk gave a shrug, picked up the young woman, carried her across the water and set her down on the other side. Then the two monks continued on their way down the road.

Though they walked in silence, the young monk was furious. He thought his companion had done entirely the wrong thing by indulging that spoiled young woman. And even worse, by touching her he had broken the monks' rule. He raved and ranted in his mind as they walked over hills and through fields. Finally, he could stand it no longer. Shouting loudly, he began scolding his companion for carrying the woman across the stream. He was beside himself with anger and completely red in the face.

"Oh, dear," said the old monk. "Are you still carrying that woman? I put her down an hour ago." He gave a shrug and continued down the road.

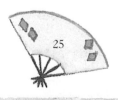

THE CONCH MAIDEN

Long, long ago, in Tibet there lived three sisters: the golden maiden, the silver maiden and the conch maiden. They were all very beautiful, and throughout the country there was not a young man who did not long to have one of them for his wife. But the golden and silver maidens were proud and fussy and thought only about how important and rich their suitors should be. Only the conch maiden wished for a husband with a good and kind heart.

One morning, the golden maiden took her golden bucket to go and fetch some water from the spring. When she opened the door, she found a beggar clothed in ugly, grubby rags lying in the dirt at the door of the house.

"What are you doing here, you filthy thing?!" screamed the golden maiden. "Away with you! Out of my sight! Be gone!"

"All right, all right, I'm going," said the beggar. "But please help me to stand up, young miss. My old legs don't work so well."

"Help yourself! Nobody told you to come here! You can leave the same way you came," said the golden maiden. "My father wants water to thin his beer. My mother needs water for her tea. I want water to wash my hair. So get moving! If you don't get out of my way, I'll step on your hand. I always do just what I want!"

No sooner said than done. She walked right over the beggar and in so doing trod on his hand. After she had passed, the beggar raised his head and looked after her with coals of fire burning in his black eyes. By the time the golden maiden came back from the spring, the beggar was gone.

The next morning, the silver maiden came out of the house carrying her silver bucket. The beggar was lying in front of the house again, and the maiden shrank back with disgust.

"How dare you lie in front of our house, you foul creature!" she cried. "Get along with you! Out of my way!"

"It's not all that easy, lovely miss," the beggar sighed. "If you only knew how my old bones hurt. Please, won't you give me a hand to stand up?"

"Oh, isn't that a fine idea!" replied the maiden in a nasty mocking voice. "My hand is the last thing you'll have! Now crawl away from here as fast as your hands and knees will carry you, or I'll step on you!"

Without waiting, she stepped over the beggar, but made sure that he got a good bang on the head from her silver bucket as

27

she passed over him. The
beggar's fiery dark eyes rested on the
maiden as she walked away. Then he was gone.

The third morning, the conch maiden went out to
fetch water. Her bucket made of conch shell sparkled
in the sun and shone with all the colors of the rainbow.
When the maiden saw the beggar lying at the door, she
stopped in her tracks.

"Would it be possible for you to make a little room for me
to get by?" she asked shyly.

"I'd like to," said the beggar, "but my old bones hurt so much I'll never be
able to get up by myself."

"Come on," said the conch maiden. "I'll help you." And she gave the beggar
her hand. He was so heavy it was all she could do to get him up without falling
down herself.

"I shouldn't let him see how hard it is for me to lift him," the maiden thought.
"Otherwise, he might think he's being a burden on me, and that might hurt his
feelings." So she smiled and chattered away in a kindly way: "See there, upsy-
daisy, no problem at all. You're just a bit frozen from lying on the cold ground.
Soon you'll be as good as ever."

"How sweet and kind you are," said the beggar. "It's almost more than a man
can believe. For your kindness, I wish you the richest husband in the land."

"Let him be rich, let him be poor; the main thing is for him to have a good
heart," the maiden said, smiling again.

28

"That might be possible, too," the beggar murmured half to himself, but with a gleam in his eye, and limped slowly behind the maiden. When she reached the spring, she knelt on the ground and began filling her bucket with water.

"Wait, let me help you," said the beggar when she tried lifting the bucket into the sling on her back. But he was so clumsy about it, all the water spilled on to the ground.

The maiden laughed. "Oh, don't bother about that. How many times I've done the same thing myself!"

They filled the bucket again, and the beggar lifted it so it could be slipped into the sling. But he held it too low for her to bend to get under it, so she said, "If it isn't too hard for you, could you lift it just a little bit higher?"

"Gladly," said the beggar. But now he lifted the bucket too high, so she still couldn't get it into the sling.

"Don't be angry with me," said the conch maiden, "but now you've got it too high for me."

"No bother at all," said the beggar. "We'll just fix that." But now when he lowered the bucket, he let it tip and the water spilled out all over the maiden's back.

"Oh no, I'm so clumsy!" the beggar cried.

"Not at all," said the maiden. "You're not clumsy. That could happen to anybody."

The beggar gave the maiden a long, thoughtful look. Again they filled the bucket with water but as he lifted it, he made an awkward movement, and the bucket slipped from his grasp and crashed to the ground, shattering into a thousand pieces. At this the conch maiden finally lost control of herself and began to cry bitterly.

"Oh, it's so sad, my beautiful bucket, my beautiful bucket!" she sobbed. But still through her tears, she said to the beggar, "Don't blame yourself. You were doing the best you could. But, oh, my parents are going to be so angry with me!" she went on crying. "A bucket made of conch is very hard to get."

29

"Perhaps I can help you after all," the beggar said softly with a little smile. Quickly and gracefully, he bent down and gathered all the shining pieces together into a little pile and began fitting them back together again. His hands moved very fast, then faster and faster. Finally they were moving so fast the maiden couldn't see them at all. Before she even had time to think, there before her eyes was her beautiful conch bucket all perfect and new, full of fresh, clean water from the spring. And the beggar showed no sign of clumsiness now when he lifted it on to her back. It seemed to slip into the sling almost all by itself. The conch maiden looked at the beggar with wonder.

"Can you do something for me?" the beggar then asked in a full, strong voice.

"Anything in my power," the maiden cried. "I'm so grateful to you for putting my bucket back together."

"Then please ask your parents to let me spend the night in your kitchen."

"Oh, I don't know if my mother would allow that," said the conch maiden timidly. "She doesn't like beggars. But I'll ask her anyway."

"In exchange, she can keep what she finds at the bottom of the bucket," said the beggar with a smile.

That aroused the maiden's curiosity. What could there be at the bottom of the bucket? There was something strange and special about all this. Somehow she knew the old man was no ordinary beggar. Despite herself, she even thought there must be something wonderful about him.

She carried her bucket of water home and asked her mother to let the beggar spend the night in the kitchen.

"You're not talking about that awful beggar that has been hanging around the door for days now, are you?" she replied crossly. The conch maiden hung her head without replying and poured the water from her bucket into a big copper tub. To her surprise there was a clank as something hit the bottom of the tub, and when she looked in, there was a small object glittering in the water. The mother quickly stuck her hand into the water and came up with a heavy ring of gold. Then the conch maiden remembered what the beggar had told her.

"That's supposed to be payment for a night's lodging," she quickly said.

"A beggar who pays in gold? That's a strange thing," said the mother. "All right, he can sleep in the kitchen."

In the evening, the whole family gathered together as usual. The father drank tea with butter in it, the way people do in Tibet, the mother spun wool and the daughters sat together laughing and talking. After a while, they began talking about suitors.

"I want to marry the Prince of India at least," declared the golden maiden. "Otherwise, I won't marry at all."

"Our own prince would be enough for me," said the silver maiden.

31

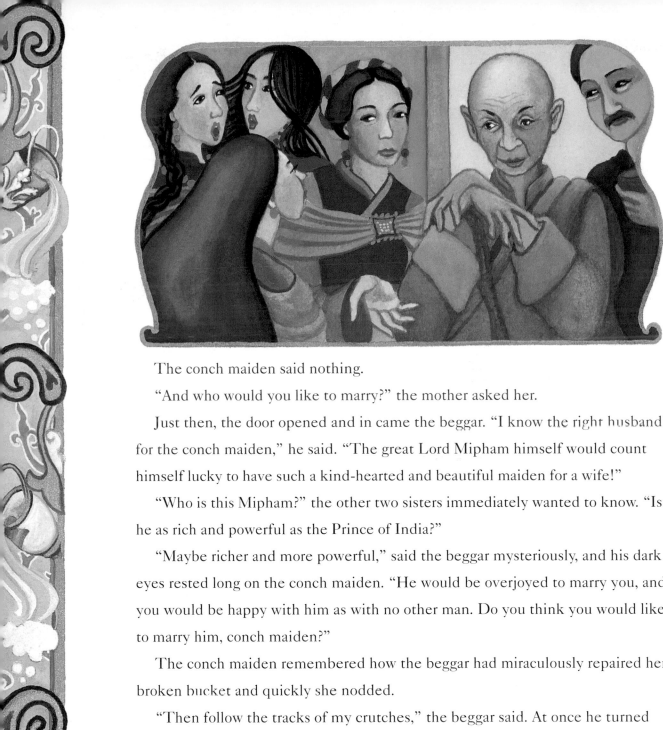

The conch maiden said nothing.

"And who would you like to marry?" the mother asked her.

Just then, the door opened and in came the beggar. "I know the right husband for the conch maiden," he said. "The great Lord Mipham himself would count himself lucky to have such a kind-hearted and beautiful maiden for a wife!"

"Who is this Mipham?" the other two sisters immediately wanted to know. "Is he as rich and powerful as the Prince of India?"

"Maybe richer and more powerful," said the beggar mysteriously, and his dark eyes rested long on the conch maiden. "He would be overjoyed to marry you, and you would be happy with him as with no other man. Do you think you would like to marry him, conch maiden?"

The conch maiden remembered how the beggar had miraculously repaired her broken bucket and quickly she nodded.

"Then follow the tracks of my crutches," the beggar said. At once he turned and hobbled out the door. The conch maiden didn't hesitate for a second, but jumped up from her chair and ran out the door after him.

"Where are you going?" her mother screamed after her. "Have you gone crazy? A beggar will only lead you to another beggar."

But it was too late. The maiden was already gone. Outside, she looked for the beggar, but all she could see was the trail of little holes in the ground made by his crutches. There was nothing for her to do but follow them, so off she ran over the hill into the darkness.

All through the night, the conch maiden followed the crutch tracks by the light of the moon, until the sky began to grow pale with dawn. Then she saw a big meadow ahead of her. On the meadow was a shepherd boy, watching over thousands of sheep.

"Did a beggar come by here?" asked the conch maiden.

"No, only Lord Mipham came by," replied the boy. "These sheep belong to him."

The maiden ran on until she came to a huge herd of yaks. "Did you see a beggar come this way?" she asked the man herding the yaks.

"No beggar," said the yak herd, "but Lord Mipham passed by a little while ago. These are his yaks."

"Where could the beggar have gone?" the maiden thought. "He might turn out to be this Lord Mipham, and then I'll end up married to a crippled old beggar." But still she went on running until she came to a large plain filled with horses.

"Have you seen a beggar?" she asked the man herding the horses.

"No, I only saw Lord Mipham, who came this way not long ago. All these horses are his."

33

Just then the sun came up over the horizon and in the morning light the maiden saw a sight that stopped her in her tracks. There before her was a golden castle, glinting and glittering in the first rays of the sun. At the castle door was an old man with white hair, who smiled at her.

"Is this the Buddha's temple?" the conch maiden asked the old man, for she could think of nothing else that could be so wonderful and magnificent as this.

"No, this is Lord Mipham's castle. Our master is waiting for you," the old man told her.

The conch maiden gathered her courage and went forward. With every step she took towards the castle, fragrant flowers grew in her footprints. By the time she reached it, a carpet of blossoms lay behind her. A handsome youth met her at the door. His dark eyes sparkled with joy. He took her gently by the hand and said, "I am Mipham. And I am the old beggar, too. Will you have me for your husband, as you said you would?" The conch maiden gazed at the handsome young man with rapture. Her heart was ready to burst with happiness. She nodded as though in a dream, and Mipham led her into the castle.

There, his servants dressed the conch maiden in a white gown that shone with all the colors of the rainbow when she moved, and adorned her with coral and glittering gems. Then she took her seat on a golden throne next to Mipham. Together they picked a date for their wedding, which took place very soon after. And since Mipham and the conch maiden both had kind and good hearts, they lived happily ever after.

THE WISDOM
OF THE CROWS

There comes a time in the life of every kind of creature when they have to go out on their own and join the company of their elders. Crows are no exception.

It happened one day that the elder crows were testing three young ones to see if they had reached the age where they had the wit and maturity to fly with their elders. To the first of the young ones, the leader of the crows put the following question: "In this whole world, what do you think crows should fear the most?"

The young crow thought a moment and then answered, "The most fearsome thing is an arrow, for it can kill a crow with one strike."

When the elder crows heard this, they thought it was a very clever answer. They flapped their wings and cawed with approval. "You speak the truth," said the leader. "We welcome you into the flock."

Then she asked the second young crow, "What do you think we should most fear?"

"I think a skilled archer is more to be feared than an arrow," the young one said, "for only the archer can aim and shoot the arrow. Without the archer, the arrow is no more than a stick, like the twig I am perching on."

The crows thought this was one of the most intelligent comments they had ever heard. The parents of the second young crow croaked with pride and beamed at their brilliant child. The leader said, "You speak with great intelligence. We are pleased to have you as a member of the flock."

Then she asked the third young crow, "And what do you think is the thing most to be feared in the world?"

"Neither of the things mentioned already," responded the young bird. "The thing in the world most to be feared is an unskillful archer."

Here was a strange answer! The bewildered crows stood about silent and embarrassed. Many thought the third young crow was simply not bright enough to understand the question. "Why do you say a thing like that?" the leader of the flock finally asked.

"The second of my companions is right. Without the archer, there is nothing to fear from an arrow. But a skilled archer's arrow will fly where it is aimed. So when you hear the twang of the bowstring, you only have to fly to one side or the other, and his arrow will miss you for sure. But with an unskilled archer, you never know where his arrow will go. If you try to get away, you may fly right into its path. You never can know whether to move or stay still."

When the birds heard this, they knew that the third young crow had real wisdom, which sees beyond the surface of things. They spoke of him with admiration and respect. Not long afterwards, they asked him to become the leader of the flock.

37

THE STONE APE

Many years ago, in a time long past, there was a beautiful island, which lay right in the middle of the Great Eastern Sea. The name of the island was Mountain of Flowers and Fruits, and on it was a large rock.

Since the beginning of the world, this rock had absorbed all the secret powers of heaven and earth and sun and moon, so by the time this story begins, it was full of magic.

One day, the rock split open, and out came a stone egg. After a while, the egg hatched, and out of it jumped a little stone ape. He bowed to the four corners of the earth—east, south, west and north—and then ran off bursting with energy and joy.

The stone ape grew up willful and strong. When he played with the other apes of the island, he was always in charge of the games and adventures. One day, he led the whole tribe to swim and bathe in a clear, blue pool. As they approached the pool, they heard a great roaring sound. They looked up and saw that the

sound came from a waterfall that fell into the pool from a cliff high above.

"Look at the waterfall!" cried one of the apes. "Whoever can pass through it shall be our king!"

"I can do it!" exclaimed the stone ape, and bounded over to the waterfall. He closed his eyes, gathered his strength and leapt through the swiftly falling water. When he opened his eyes he saw before him an iron bridge. Beyond the bridge was the entrance to a cave of great splendor and beauty. It was big and high, and inside were rock formations of wondrous colors. It was called Heavenly Cave.

After exploring the cave, the stone ape went back over the bridge, leapt back through the curtain of falling water and landed among the other apes. He told them of the beautiful cave that lay on the other side of the waterfall. When they understood what he had found, they became very excited and all began to jabber at once. They begged the stone ape to lead them to the cave.

"Follow me!" he shouted. He jumped back through the water and, with him in the lead, the others had the courage to jump too. One by one they came through behind him, and they all went over the bridge to the cave.

So it happened that the stone ape became the king of the apes. He and his subjects lived in happiness and contentment in Heavenly Cave for over three hundred years.

During these years, the stone ape was continually learning new things. He became more and more intelligent until he grew as intelligent as a human being. And as he became smarter and smarter, he also became more and more curious. Soon he began to

learn unusual things, and he became the master of seventy-two different kinds of miraculous powers. He could take the shape of anything he wished—human, plant, animal or mineral; he could ride clouds as if they were horses; and he was not afraid of any being or thing.

This was all very well and good, except that the stone ape used his powers only for his own amusement and glory and didn't seem to care how much trouble he made for others.

Now the stone ape had a magic iron rod, which he had stolen from the palace of the dragon king under the sea, and this rod was a very powerful weapon. He used it to fight his way into the underworld, the realm of the dead. There he forced the ten princes of the dead to give him the book of life and death. This book held the names of every creature and the number of years each had to live. He looked through the book until he found the page where his own name was written. He tore the page out and crumpled it in his hand. Now the stone ape would never die.

Just to make sure of this, he stole into the Western Heaven, where the sage Lao-tzu lived, who brewed the elixir of eternal life. As wise as Lao-tzu was, it took him a long time to make just a little of this elixir, and just one drop was enough to make a being live for ever.

The stone ape found five gourds filled with the elixir and drained them all to the bottom. "Now I will surely live forever!" he shouted with joy. Then to escape the wrath of the gods, he made himself invisible and crept out of the western gate of that heaven. "Now I'll go back to earth and rule as king," said the stone ape to himself.

Another time, he stole the peaches of Hei-wang-mu, the mother of the fairies. These were no ordinary peaches. They grew only in the fairy mother's orchard,

40

and only once every three thousand years. And once every three thousand years, when the trees were laden down with fruit, the fairy mother would invite all the gods and fairies to her orchard to feast on the magical peaches.

Now on the very day of the fairy mother's peach party, before the guests arrived, the stone ape stole into the orchard and stuffed himself with all the peaches he could possibly eat. By the time he had finished, he was so full and heavy that he just had to lie down to sleep. He thought to himself, "If the fairy mother and her guests should come, I won't be able to run away!" So he turned himself into a tiny little peach worm, crawled under the bark of one of the trees and fell asleep. When the gods and fairies came and found their feast spoiled, they looked high and low for the thief, but nobody suspected the little peach worm, asleep in the tree.

Now the Lord of Heaven had been watching the stone ape and saw all the trouble he was causing. "This must stop," he thought. But as the stone ape was so wily and clever and had so many miraculous powers, it was very difficult to control him. "Only the Lord Buddha can tame him now," the Lord of Heaven concluded. So he sent a messenger to the Buddha and respectfully requested him to do something to keep the stone ape from wreaking havoc in heaven and on earth.

The Lord Buddha came out of the West. When he saw him, the stone ape shouted at him, "Who are you that dares to disturb me?!" The Buddha looked at him calmly. "I am the Buddha," he said, "and I am here to tame you."

"Do you know to whom you are speaking?" said the stone ape, full of pride and defiance. "I am the stone ape. I am a king. I hold the hidden knowledge. I am master of seventy-two different kinds of miraculous powers and the holder of eternal life! I am afraid of no one, certainly not you!"

The Buddha smiled. "I've heard that you can somersault over the clouds and that each somersault takes you a thousand miles. Can you really do that? If you can, show me."

"I can do anything!" shouted the stone ape. And off he went, somersaulting through the sky. He went head over heels so fast and so many times, he became like a whirlwind, high up beyond the clouds. He continued for a long, long time, covering an immense distance with every turn. Finally, he came to what seemed like the edge of the sky, where he saw five huge, red pillars. They were very tall and disappeared into the sky above. "My goodness!" he thought. "I must have reached the end of the world!" He was very proud of himself. To show he had been there, he somersaulted up to the middle pillar and made his mark on it. Then he somersaulted back to where he had started. The Buddha was waiting for him.

"Well, not only can I somersault a thousand miles at a time, but I have somersaulted to the end of the world!" he boasted. "If you don't believe me, go have a look for yourself. I left my mark on one of the pillars."

"Perhaps you should have a look at this," said the Buddha and held up his hand. On the Buddha's middle finger the stone ape saw the mark he had made on the pillar at the end of the world. He was stunned and afraid. The whole time he was somersaulting, he was in the palm of the Buddha's hand!

The stone ape realized he had met his master and he tried to escape. But the Buddha put his hand down over him. Then he made a magic mountain out of the basic elements of the world—water, fire, wood, earth and metal—and put it over the stone ape. Try as he would, using all his miraculous powers, the stone ape was unable to escape from beneath the magic mountain. At last earth and heaven were safe from his mischief.

The apes say that after a thousand years beneath the magic mountain, the stone ape reappeared on the island. They say that time brought about in him a change of heart, and nowadays, though he still has lots of fun, he uses his intelligence and powers to help others.

WHERE ARE YOU GOING?

Zen teachers encourage their young pupils to outsmart each other in battles of wits. One pupil will keep asking questions till he can get a second one to say something stupid. The pupils become very careful about how they answer even a simple question, because they do not want to get trapped in their own words.

Two Zen temples that were near each other each used to send a pupil to market every morning to buy vegetables. Each day, the two children met on the way.

"Where are you going?" one little boy asked the other one morning.

"I am going wherever my feet take me," answered the second.

This answer stumped the first boy. He could not think of another question that might confuse the second boy in any way. When he returned from the market, he told his teacher what had happened.

44

"Tomorrow," said the teacher, "ask him the same question. He'll say the same thing, and then you can mix him up by saying, 'Suppose you had no feet. Where are you going?'"

Next morning, the first boy asked, "Where are you going?"

The second boy answered, "Wherever the wind blows."

The first boy was puzzled again. He couldn't think of a thing to say. When he got home, he told his teacher about his second defeat.

"Tomorrow, ask him where he would be going if there was no wind," his teacher told him.

The next day, the boys met for the third time.

"Where are you going?" asked the first boy.

"I'm going to the market to buy vegetables," said the second boy.

45

ANGULIMALA THE BRIGAND

Thousands of years ago, in the land of India, there was a prosperous kingdom called Kosala. The king's name was Prasenajit and his palace was in the glittering city of Shravasti, which was full of splendid shops, beautiful parks and magnificent mansions.

All was well and happy in the kingdom of Kosala until a terrible blight fell upon it. It was not the usual kind of catastrophe—a flood, famine, plague or war. Rather, it was all caused by one man, a fearsome brigand, whose name was Angulimala, which means "finger necklace." This is because he had made a vow to kill a thousand people, and to keep count, he saved a finger from each of his victims and wore it on a cord around his neck.

No one could stop Angulimala. The king's men could never catch him because he could run faster than the fastest horse and he was tremendously strong and very clever. Once a party of forty men on horseback went out to catch

him, and he killed them all and strung their fingers on his necklace. Whole villages in the countryside became empty as all the people took refuge in the city out of fear of Angulimala. No one went out of doors at night for fear of Angulimala, and even during the day people stayed far, far away from the part of the country where he lived.

Now, at that time, it so happened that the great teacher called the Buddha, whose name means "the awakened one," was also living in Kosala near the city of Shravasti. He was called "the awakened one" because he had awakened from all the hopes and fears that torment human beings and keep them lost in a kind of dream. When they are happy, they hope to be happier and are afraid to lose the happiness they have. When they are unhappy, they fear they will remain that way. They blame other people for their problems and somehow hope to get out of them that way. But the Buddha had awakened from all that. He was content to be just as he was.

The Buddha lived as a monk, without any money or possessions. Every morning, after he had spent some time sitting calmly and peacefully without thinking about anything (which is called meditating), he would walk into the city of Shravasti to beg for his morning meal—his only meal of the day. He would start at the end of a street and go around to the back of each house, to the kitchen door, and stand there with his begging bowl without saying anything. India is a very hot country, so people kept their kitchen doors open. They would see the monk standing at the door, and if they had any extra food they would put some in his bowl. Everyone knew the Buddha was an awakened person, so when people saw him they felt honored that he had come to their house, and he usually didn't have much trouble collecting a bowlful of food.

47

One particular morning, as he was on his begging round in Shravasti, he heard people complaining bitterly about Angulimala. They said that a great number of people were going to King Prasenajit's palace to demand that the king take his army and go out and catch the fearsome, invincible brigand. After hearing this, the Buddha carried his bowl of food back to his sleeping place, ate quietly and put his things in order. Then he set out along the road that led to where Angulimala lived.

As he walked along, the Buddha met people coming in the other direction. "Do not go that way, monk," they told him. "Angulimala lives down there. Anybody who goes in that direction is sure to get killed."

The Buddha listened politely to what they said, but then continued on his way in silence. At first, there were quite a few passersby going in the opposite direction who gave the Buddha this warning. But the closer he got to Angulimala's lair, the fewer people were on the road. At last, except for him, the road was completely deserted. The Buddha continued walking quietly along.

Up on the hill in the forest, Angulimala saw the Buddha coming. "How amazing!" thought the brigand. "He can't have heard of me. People don't dare come this close even in groups of a hundred armed men—and here comes this unarmed monk all by himself. Wonderful! In a few minutes, I shall have another finger for my necklace, and with hardly any trouble at all!"

So saying, the brigand picked up his bow and arrows and buckled on his sword. Swiftly and nimbly, he ran down through the trees. Without making a

sound, he came out on to the road a short distance behind the Buddha.

Then a strange thing happened. Angulimala couldn't catch up with the Buddha. As we know, Angulimala was a very fast runner, faster than a horse or a deer, but no matter how fast and long he ran, the Buddha was always just out of his reach. And the strangest thing was that the Buddha himself was not running at all. He was just walking along at his normal pace.

Angulimala could not understand this, and he became more and more furious at being unable to get his hands on the Buddha. He ran and ran, panting and sweating, panting and sweating. He ran until at last he could run no more. Then he stopped in his tracks and shouted at the Buddha, "Stop, monk, stop, stop!"

The Buddha kept walking quietly along, but now the amazing thing was that although the brigand had stopped completely, the distance between them grew no greater.

"I have stopped," said the Buddha, turning his head to look the brigand in the eye. "Now, you should stop too."

"What do you mean by that?!" shouted the infuriated brigand, who thought things were just the other way around.

"I've stopped living in dreams of hope and fear and so I have stopped hating and harming others. So instead of being stuck as you are, I can move just as I please. Now, listen, Angulimala: if you want to be able to go as you like as I can, you should stop too."

When Angulimala heard these words and looked at the Buddha, who was

49

gazing at him kindly from just beyond his reach, walking calmly along without getting any further away, suddenly he realized how stupidly wrong he'd been all those years. He wished with all his heart that he'd never done harm to anyone. He took off his weapons and threw them in the ditch. Then he fell on his knees and asked the Buddha to help him.

"You can come along with me and be a monk," said the Buddha. "I'll teach you how to meditate. Keep your heart open the way it is now, and everything will be just fine."

So the Buddha walked back into Shravasti with Angulimala walking humbly at his heels. They went to the Jeta Grove, a park in the city where the Buddha often stayed with his followers. Not long after they got there, King Prasenajit arrived with five hundred soldiers. "We're going after Angulimala," said the king. "But I'm afraid we're going to have a difficult time, so I have come to ask your advice."

"Good," said the Buddha. "Why don't you sit down and have a cup of tea and we'll talk about it?"

The king was anxious to seek the Buddha's help, so he sat down near him on the ground. The Buddha beckoned to Angulimala, who had by now changed his clothes and was wearing a simple monk's robe. He took him to one side and spoke to him softly. And so, when the water was ready, following the instructions the Buddha had just given him, the once fearsome brigand, Angulimala, served the Buddha and the king tea.

"What would you do," said the Buddha to the king as they sipped their tea, "if you discovered that Angulimala had become a simple monk, without possessions, devoted to a life of meditation and doing good for others?"

"To begin with, I'd be really amazed," said the king. "But if it really happened, I suppose I would pardon him and treat him with the respect due to a monk."

"Good," said the Buddha, "because that is Angulimala who has served you tea."

The king jumped up, white with fear and anger. But the Buddha soothed him, explaining that Angulimala had really changed and no one need be afraid of him anymore. After he had had a few minutes to get used to the new situation, the king let go of his bad feelings and began to feel really quite pleased. Then he took leave of the Buddha, explaining that he had other things to do, and he and his army all went home.

Angulimala became a very eager follower of the Buddha and spent a lot of time in the forest meditating according to his master's instructions. As sometimes happens to people who meditate a lot, after a while he began to develop special abilities which he used to help other people. Angulimala seemed to have a special talent for helping mothers give birth to their children. Whenever there was a problem with a birth, Angulimala was always called. It seemed he only had to be there for everything to go smoothly. So although many people remembered his bad deeds of earlier days and turned away from him when he was on his begging rounds, there were always enough grateful mothers or mothers-to-be, and Angulimala usually received enough to eat, so he could go back to the forest and meditate.

But when anyone has done as much evil as Angulimala had, killing all those people, there are bound to be bad results. After a few years, when the former brigand went to the city to beg, he began to have accidents. If a flowerpot fell off

a windowsill, it would hit Angulimala. If anywhere near him someone was beating an animal, somehow the blows all landed on Angulimala. If someone threw a stone at someone else in anger, it hit Angulimala. Any time one person used a weapon on another, instead of hitting the intended person it hit Angulimala. And it got worse and worse.

Finally, bruised and broken and only half alive, Angulimala dragged himself to the Buddha and begged him for help and advice.

The Buddha told him: "Young man, gather your courage and hold out for a while longer. Though you may not think so, this is the very best thing that could be happening. All those murders you committed had to be paid for. If you had not changed your ways, you would have been reborn again and again and experienced terrible punishments in all your future lives. But since you have worked so hard to make your heart pure and have done so much to help other people, all your bad deeds are ripening now. If you can stand it just a little longer, it will be over. Your debt will be paid."

So Angulimala took heart and he endured the painful accidents a while longer. Gradually they happened less and less and finally stopped altogether. Angulimala went on meditating in the forest and giving his help whenever it was needed to mothers in childbirth. He lived a long time and came to be admired and even loved by the very people who once hated and feared him. Gradually, like the Buddha, he awoke entirely from his dream of hope and fear and became completely fearless and wholly contented.

LEARNING TO BE SILENT

A group of four friends were all studying meditation. They decided, in order to clear their minds, to take a vow of silence and not talk for seven days. The first day, they meditated all day without saying a word. But when night fell and the oil lamps in the meditation hall grew dim, one of the friends whispered to a servant, "Take care of those lamps."

One of the others, shocked to hear his friend speaking, said, "You are not supposed to be talking!"

The third one was overcome with irritation. "You idiots!" he said. "Why did you talk?"

"I am the only one who hasn't talked," said the fourth friend, smiling proudly.

GOODHEART AND THE
GODDESS OF THE FOREST

Once there lived a rich merchant who had three sons. The elder two sons had already long ago brought home well-to-do brides; only the youngest didn't seem to want to think about marriage. He spent all his time hanging around the town being friendly to the poor and giving them money. That is why everybody called him Goodheart.

But his two elder brothers and their wives were not happy about Goodheart's behavior, because he was giving away the family money. One day, the brothers went to their father and said, "Don't you see how carelessly our brother is giving away our money? Soon our entire fortune will be gone. You should throw him out of the house." The father agreed and sent for his youngest son.

"Your brothers have been complaining about you," he said. "You've been giving our money thoughtlessly to the poor, and soon we'll all be beggars ourselves.

What you need is to go out into the world and learn how hard it is to earn a living. On top of that, it's high time you found a wife and got married." Then he gave the youth a horse, three gold coins and his blessing to send him on his way. Goodheart thanked his father, said goodbye to his brothers and rode out of the town towards the south.

He wandered for days and weeks. Before long he gave his gold coins away. Then he sold his horse. He ate whatever he found or kind people gave him, and he slept wherever he was at the end of the day, mostly on the ground under the stars. He passed through many towns, always going south. One day he came to a part of the country where there were no more people or houses. He walked the whole day without meeting a single person or getting anything to eat. It grew dark, and he could not see a light in any direction. He seemed to have become lost in a very empty place, and he was afraid.

All at once, out of nowhere, an old man with white hair appeared in front of him. "Good evening," said Goodheart and bowed to the old man. "Are you from this place? I'm lost and I'm looking for somewhere to spend the night."

"I have come to give you a piece of advice," said the old man and smiled mysteriously. "Stop traveling south. Go north. Go north until you come to the edge of a forest. There you wil find a fir tree with a slender trunk. Sit down under it and wait. When evening comes, it will begin to shiver and sigh, and then it will turn into a beautiful goddess. Then don't hesitate for an instant, but take hold of her by the hem of her dress and ask her to be your wife."

Then the old man disappeared as suddenly as if he had been swallowed by the earth. Goodheart lay down and went to sleep. The next day, he began walking north. He walked until he came to the edge of the forest and found a place where there was a fir tree with a slender trunk. He sat down and leaned his head against it and waited. Night fell and the moon began to rise. As moonlight touched the forest, the trunk shivered and the tree gave a deep sigh. Before Goodheart's eyes, it turned into a beautiful goddess, who looked at him and smiled.

Goodheart fell in love with the goddess as soon as his eyes met hers. He took hold of the hem of her dress and said, "O beautiful woman, please don't ever leave me. Please stay with me always and be my wife."

"You ask much," said the goddess, "yet so it is to be." And she gave him her hand.

"I am poor," said the youth. "I have nothing but my hands, but I will do everything to make us happy."

"Let that be my worry too," laughed the goddess. She unknotted her green headcloth and tossed it back over the top of her head. In an instant in front of them stood a lovely, snug little hut with the table already set in front of the hearth. Oh, how happy the young couple were!

But after they had eaten, the goddess said, "We can't stay here longer than three days. Whatever shall we do then?"

Before Goodheart could utter a word in reply, a messenger arrived and announced, "The goddess's father commands Goodheart to come immediately and split wood for him."

The goddess took the youth by the

hand and whispered to him, "That's what I was afraid of. My father is the forest giant. He wants to test you. He has three huge piles of firewood lying in his yard, but no mortal man can chop that wood. Take this axe and swing it three times over each heap."

Goodheart took the axe and went to the giant's yard, and there he found three huge heaps of wood that was as hard as stone. Goodheart swung the axe over each heap three times, and an invisible hand chopped the wood into little pieces. In no more than an instant, the wood was split and neatly piled.

"Oh-ho," said the giant, "you're not a bad fellow. But you won't win my daughter that easily. Tomorrow her mother wants to see you."

Goodheart went home to the goddess and told her everything.

"Oh, that's awful!" said the goddess. "My mother is the forest witch. A visit to her can only end badly. I'm

going to give you a magic sword, and when you go into her hut tomorrow, hold up the sword and keep the blade between you and her."

The next morning, Goodheart went to visit the witch. When he entered her room, he saw an ugly hag sitting on a sooty stove. She cackled and her eyes rolled in her head and glittered wildly. Goodheart drew the sword and held it up to the weird woman. At once she turned into a green snake from whose fangs little tongues of flame streamed out. The snake leapt into the air, opened its huge jaws and fell upon the youth. But he stuck his sword deep into its throat and killed it.

"My father will never forgive us," said the goddess when Goodheart had told her the story. "We have to run for it." So the two young people joined hands and started running away as fast as they could. They hadn't gotten far when they heard a dreadful noise behind them. They were being chased by thousands of green spirits, who were flitting through the air and shrieking hideously. At their head rode the giant, mounted on a strange animal and howling as he came.

"Keep running!" the goddess cried out to Goodheart. "If I win, I'll catch up with you along the way. If I lose, we'll never see each other again." Then she drew a sword from her sleeve, leapt onto a cloud and flew straight at the ghastly horde.

"Miserable creature! You've bound yourself to a mortal and destroyed your own mother. You'll be sorry!" the voice of the giant thundered out of the cloud.

There was a fierce battle. Sword clattered on sword and there were many screams and cries. The goddess fought with deadly courage and finally she put the horde of green spirits to flight. As the noise of the battle died away, the sky cleared. There was just one white cloud in the sky, which was sailing gently down to earth. The goddess jumped from the cloud, unknotted her green headcloth and tossed it back over the top of her head. In an instant, she changed into a white stallion and galloped away after Goodheart.

When the stallion appeared next to the youth, he grabbed it by the tail, swung himself up on its back and trotted into the nearby town. There he met a magician who was disguised as a merchant. The magician had only to glance at the beautiful white stallion to know it was no ordinary horse. He told Goodheart he was a horse dealer and offered him another horse, complete with saddle, for the stallion and a bag of gold coins into the bargain.

"That's a deal!" said Goodheart and gave the stallion to the magician.

"And now let's see what this horse really is," said the magician when he got home. He fired up his stove, and when it was so hot that flames were licking out of the chimneytop, he pushed the horse into the oven. But as soon as he closed the oven door, it popped open again and out flew a little bird.

"Wait till I catch you!" shouted the magician in a rage. He turned himself into a hawk and flew after the little bird. He was just about to catch the little creature, when it changed into a golden ring and fell to the ground in the midst of a crowd of playing children.

"That's a pretty ring!" cried one of the children and ran home with it to put it in his special box.

But the magician got there first and met him at the door. "Give me that ring!" he snapped.

"No, it's mine!" said the child.

"No, it's mine! I lost it. It's got my sign on it." Then he snatched the ring out of the child's hand.

"Now you won't get away," gloated the magician, looking down at the ring in his hand. But at the same moment it slipped from his grasp and fell to the ground. The magician got down on his hands and knees and looked everywhere, but no matter how hard he looked, he couldn't find it.

"Look all you like, you'll never find me!" called a voice above his head. The magician looked up in time to see a white cloud sailing away with the forest goddess on it, laughing at him.

Now the goddess raced like the wind after Goodheart. When she caught up with him, she jumped from the cloud and said, "So I was to be your wife, but I changed myself into a white stallion so I could become your wife; then you went and sold me to a magician which almost cost me my life!"

"Don't be angry, darling goddess," said Goodheart. "I didn't know it was you." He took her by the hand and took her home with him. What a joy it was when the youngest son returned home with his beautiful bride! They immediately invited all their family and friends to their wedding. The two elder brothers came, and there was also an old uncle, who had one hen eye and one cock eye. The uncle looked the wives of the two older brothers over with approval, but he couldn't take his gaze off Goodheart's beautiful bride. Something seemed to him not quite right about her.

The wives of the elder brothers could only carry one bowl at a time when it came to serving the guests, but Goodheart's bride always brought several. In the kitchen, she was a marvel. The food seemed to turn into wonderfully cooked meals all by itself.

"There's something strange here," thought the uncle. He shut his hen eye tight and looked at her piercingly with his cock eye. After a while, he said to himself, "She's not from this world." He took Goodheart's father aside and said, "Look, brother, this is none of my business, but there's something I don't like about the bride. It wouldn't do to have an evil spirit in the family. You'd better throw her out of the house before it's too late."

"What are you saying?!" Goodheart cried when his father told him of his uncle's suspicions. "Do you have any idea how hard and rare it is to win such a bride? I will never be parted from her."

The uncle said no more. Then the time came for his own only daughter to be married. He invited the wives of the three brothers and gave them the task of making a hundred dresses for the bride. All the dresses had to be ready in three days. The wives of the two older brothers went straight to work. But Goodheart's wife lay about the house, singing to herself and not lifting a finger. At the end of two days, the elder brothers' wives had made only five dresses each. Desperately they stared at all the bolts of cloth that still had to be made into dresses.

"Give them to me," said Goodheart's wife and carried all the cloth into her room. "Tonight, I'll do some sewing," she said.

That night, the goddess took nine candles, set them up in a row and lit them one after the other. From the flames of the burning candles, nine pillars of smoke arose. They found their way out the windows and rose higher and higher until they reached all the way up into the sky. Then nine maidens came down the pillars of smoke and set to work making dresses. First they measured and cut the

cloth. Then when the cloth was all ready, they threaded their needles with silver moonbeams and sewed the dresses with such fine stitches that no seams could be found. Before long, stacks of gorgeous dresses lay all about the room. When the last dress was done, the candles went out and the maidens disappeared.

In the morning, the uncle came and said, "So, now, ladies, have you finished your work?"

Said the older brothers' wives, "We worked as hard as we could, but we were only able to make five dresses apiece. Goodheart's wife took all the rest of the cloth."

"And how many dresses did you make?" he asked Goodheart's wife.

She pointed at the dresses all piled up in her room. "Here are ninety dresses," she said. The uncle shut his hen eye tight and, winking his cock eye very quickly once for each dress, he counted up the dresses. Now he was sure there was no mistake. This wife of Goodheart's was not from this world. But he said not a word.

One day when the goddess was alone in the house, there came a loud banging on the door. When she opened it, the uncle pushed his way into the room with a net of the kind that is used to catch spirits. The goddess knew right away what the uncle was up to, and before he could even try to catch her, he was all tangled up in his own spirit net. Then the goddess ran to Goodheart and said, "You know I come from no earthly race. I have no choice now but to leave the human world. Come with me if you want. Otherwise, we must separate for ever."

"A man and a wife should face together whatever good or evil comes to them," declared Goodheart. "I will never leave you."

"Then close your eyes and give me your hand," said the goddess. Goodheart closed his eyes, gave her his hand and at once began to feel himself flying through the air. A long time passed before he felt firm ground under his feet. As he opened his eyes, he saw the goddess unknot her green cloth and toss it back

over her head. In an instant, a small but very cozy little hut stood before them, and there they lived, happy and contented. Before a year had passed, the goddess gave birth to a beautiful son.

At the time that the little boy was taking his first steps, it happened that the imperial army was passing through the region. The soldiers saw the young woman and how beautiful she was, and they tried to carry her off as a gift to the emperor. But once again she threw her green cloth over her head. At that very instant, a white cloud floated down from the sky, took the goddess, her son and Goodheart, and flew away as the soldiers looked on in amazement.

Higher and higher and higher flew the cloud, into the depths of the sky, where it finally stopped. Since that time, the goddess and her husband and her son have lived in the sky. And whoever does not believe it has only to look up at the stars at night. If you're lucky, you'll see three lights—two big ones and a small one— that never, ever grow apart.

THE DEATH OF A TEACUP

There once was a great teacher of Zen, a school of the Buddha's teaching that is very down to earth about how the things in life really are. This great teacher's name was Ikkyu. Even as a young boy he was very clever and always found a way of getting himself out of trouble.

One day as he was playing, Ikkyu knocked over a teacup, which fell to the floor and shattered into pieces. Now the teacup belonged to his teacher, and it was very old and precious, and his teacher valued it greatly. As Ikkyu was worrying about this accident, he heard his teacher coming and quickly hid the pieces of the cup behind his back. When his teacher appeared, Ikkyu asked him, "Why do people die?"

"That is just natural," his teacher replied. "Everything only has so long to live, and then it must die."

At these words, Ikkyu showed his teacher the pieces of the broken teacup.

68

69

THE FOOLISH BOY

There once was a boy who lived with his poor mother in a small cottage. As the boy grew up, he was found to be rather weak-minded. He was continually getting into trouble because he was so simple. The other children made fun of him by getting him to believe the most outrageous stories.

One day, he went for a walk in a field full of yellow spring flowers—barefoot, of course, since he had no shoes. He was sitting among the flowers when another boy passed and called to him, "Hey, do you know that the soles of your feet have turned all yellow? That's a sure sign you're going to die right away."

The poor foolish boy was very frightened, but he thought to himself, "If I am going to die, then I'll need a grave." So he began digging. Pretty soon he had made a shallow hole. He lay down in it and began waiting to die.

Just then, one of the king's servants came by carrying a big earthenware jar full of oil for the king. He saw the boy lying in the hole and asked him what he was doing.

"The soles of my feet have turned yellow, and as you know, that's a sure sign I'm about to die. So I've made myself a little grave and I'm waiting."

"That's ridiculous!" said the king's servant. "You couldn't talk to me like that if you were dying. Why don't you get out of that hole and do something useful? Look, help me carry this jar of oil to the king, and in return I'll give you a hen."

So the foolish boy climbed out of the hole, lifted the big jar of oil on to his back and started off for the palace with the king's servant. As they went along, the boy thought about what he would do with the hen he was going to get.

"When the hen lays eggs, I'll let her hatch them," he thought. "I should end up with quite a few chicks. When the chicks grow up into cocks and hens, I'll sell them at the market. Then I'll take the money and buy a cow. Then the cow will have a calf, and I'll sell both the cow and the calf and buy a nice little house. Once I have a house, I'll be able to get married. Then my wife and I will have a baby. When the child grows up, I'll have to make sure it behaves properly. If it's good and does what it's told, I'll be very kind to it. But if it's disobedient, I shall be very firm with it and stamp my foot, just like this!"

And the boy stamped his foot so hard that the jar slipped off his back and smashed to bits on the ground. When the king's servant saw the broken jar and the spilled oil, he lost his temper.

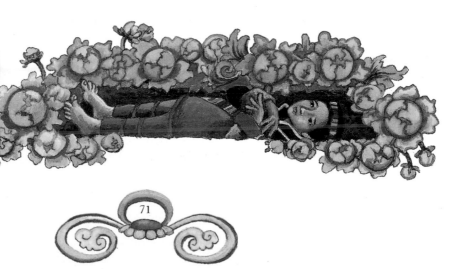

"What do you mean by stamping your foot like that and spilling the king's oil?!" he screamed. The boy felt he could explain everything, but when he tried, the servant lost patience, took him by the ear and dragged him off to the king.

"Your Majesty, I tried to get this boy to help carry your oil. But as we were walking along, suddenly he started stamping his foot like a maniac. The jar slipped off his back and broke into a hundred pieces!"

The king asked the boy to explain his behavior.

"Well, your Majesty," he replied, "your servant offered me a hen in payment for carrying the oil. Since I knew I was going to get a hen, it was only natural for me to plan what I would do with it. I quickly figured that by selling the chickens I could buy a cow, and then the cow would have a calf, and by selling the cow and calf, I could buy a house. Then I could get married and have a child. I had to plan how to raise the child properly. I resolved that if it was disobedient, I would have to be firm with it and stamp my foot to show it I meant business."

When the king had heard this ridiculous story, he was quite amused. He had a good laugh, gave the boy a gold coin and told him to go home to his mother.

When the boy reached his house, he saw a strange dog sneaking out the front door with a purse full of money in his mouth. He became extremely excited and began shouting to his mother that a dog was running off with her purse. When the mother saw what was happening, she was afraid the boy would attract other people with his cries and somebody else would chase the dog and get the money. So she ran up on to the roof of the house and sprinkled sugar all over it. Then she called to the boy to come up as quickly as he could.

"Look!" she said. "It's been raining sugar on the roof!"

The boy loved sugar and immediately set to work gathering it all up. With her son busy in this way, the mother slipped out of the house, quickly found the dog and got her purse back.

Some time later, the boy's mother arranged to marry the boy into a rich family who lived far enough away that they hadn't heard of the youth's simple-mindedness. The custom was for the man to go to live with the bride's family.

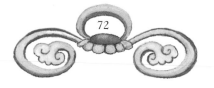

First the men of the bride's family came to the groom's house for a feast, and then they were to take the groom back home with them. The boy dressed in his best clothes, but when the feast was over, he asked the men from his bride's family to go on ahead, since he wanted to take some time to say goodbye to his mother.

At nightfall, he rode off alone by moonlight. As he went, he could see his shadow moving along beside him. He could not see it exactly, but he was afraid it was a ghost or demon, so he kicked his horse into a gallop to get away. But the faster he went, the faster his shadow went too. He saw he was not going to escape, so he grabbed his hat and threw it hard at the shadow to try to frighten it. That didn't work, so he threw his coat at it too, then his shirt, then his trousers and so on, until he didn't have a stitch left on his body. But the shadow was not frightened and continued to follow him closely. Thinking he might slip away, he jumped off his horse and began running along the road on foot. He ran till he reached the shade of a big tree that grew by the side of the road.

Once under the tree, he was overjoyed to find that the shadow had disappeared. But as soon as he peeped out from the shadow of the tree, no matter in which direction, the shadow appeared again. This was very upsetting. Finally the foolish boy decided the safest thing was to stay in the shade of the tree, so he climbed up into the branches and soon was fast asleep.

Some travelers came along the same way some time later. As they approached, they were surprised to find articles of clothing scattered along the road. They

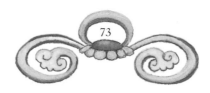

gathered them up one by one, and when they found a horse grazing by the roadside, they took that too. They came to the big tree and sat down beneath it to divide up what they had found. Just then the boy woke up and saw what was going on below. So he cried out, "What about me! I want my share too!"

Hearing a loud voice coming out of the tree, the travelers were frightened out of their wits. Thinking that it must be a demon demanding his share, they ran as fast as they could, leaving the clothes and the horse behind. The boy climbed out of the tree, put on his clothes, mounted the horse and rode off to his bride's house.

When he got there, he found he wasn't so very late. The bride's parents led him to a big room where family, friends and neighbors were waiting to begin the wedding feast. Everyone started to celebrate. There was laughing and singing and lots to eat and drink. The boy was having quite a good time, but he also found he missed his mother. He thought the least he could do was save her some of this

excellent food. He found a copper vase with a small mouth and hid it in his lap. As he ate, he kept dropping choice bits into the vase for his mother. He was putting a little cake in the vase very carefully, when his hand went in too far and got stuck. He couldn't get it out! This was quite awkward. With his hand stuck in the vase, he couldn't eat. Everybody noticed he wasn't eating and pressed him to have more. But he just sat there with his hand in his lap saying he'd had enough, though he was still very hungry.

Hours later, the guests left and the boy was left alone with his bride. She asked him what was the matter with him and why he was acting so strangely. At first, he was too shy to say anything, but finally he had to tell her the story and show her his hand stuck in the vase.

"Oh, that's not such a big problem," she said sweetly. "There's a big white stone at the foot of the stairs. Just beat the vase against the stone and it's bound to break or come off."

So the young fellow stole down the stairs in the dark and came to what looked like a big white stone near the bottom of the steps. He crept up to it, raised his arm and brought down the copper vase with all his might on the round white object. The vase broke and came off his hand, but to his horror instead of the clank he expected, he heard an awful groan. Looking closer, he found that what he had hit wasn't a stone at all. It was his white-haired father-in-law whom he had given a violent blow on the head. The poor man had drunk too much beer at the feast and fallen asleep at the foot of the stairs.

Terrified and sure that he had killed him, the boy ran out of the house into the night. After a while, he came to a farm. A large honeycomb had been left in a corner of the farmyard. Not knowing what it was, the boy lay down on it and fell asleep. He was soon smeared all over with honey. In the middle of the night, he grew cold and crawled into a shed where wool was stored. He lay down on that and slept until dawn.

When he awoke, he saw in the morning light that he was all white and woolly. "Oh, no!" thought the poor simple boy. "As a punishment for killing my father-in-law, I've been turned into a sheep!" He was very unhappy, but he ran out of the courtyard and joined a flock of sheep grazing on a nearby hillside. He spent the whole day wandering around with the sheep, trying his best to learn the customs and habits of his new companions. At night, he went with them into the enclosure where they slept.

At midnight, some robbers came. They felt around among the sheep, trying to get hold of a nice plump one. The boy was the most meaty, so one of them hoisted him up on his back and they carried him off to their hideout. They laid him on the ground and were getting ready to cut him up for their dinner when the boy became so frightened, he forgot he was supposed to be a sheep. He shouted loudly, "Please, don't kill me, kind robbers!"

Hearing a sheep with human speech, the robbers went white with fear and took to their heels. The boy was hungry and exhausted from his adventures as a sheep, so he went back to his bride's house. There he found out that the bride's father was not dead but had only been hurt. When the whole story came out, the poor youth was completely forgiven, and he settled down to live happily with his wife.

After some years, he thought he would like to make a bit of money as a trader, so he gathered some things to sell and set off for India. One night on the way, he stopped at a large inn. The innkeeper made the young man comfortable and invited him to his table for dinner. As they ate, the innkeeper told him all sorts of strange stories. Finally, the young man had to blurt out that he didn't believe him.

"To prove I'm telling the truth, tonight I'll show you something stranger than anything I've told you. I'll bet you when dark falls tonight, a cat will carry a lantern into this room."

The young man thought his host's boasting was quite silly, so he said, "All right, I'll bet you anything you like."

"Very well," said the innkeeper, "I'll bet everything I have, my house and all, against everything you have, all of your possessions."

"Fine," said the young man, quite pleased with himself. "The bet is on."

Sure enough, that evening just at twilight, a large white cat walked into the room carrying a lantern in its mouth. It seems that the innkeeper had spent a long time training it to do this, so he could trick people who stayed at his inn. So the young man had to give everything he had to the innkeeper. He had no choice but to remain at the inn as a servant.

After some months, the young man's wife became worried about him. Knowing him as she did, she was afraid he'd got himself into some kind of trouble. She decided to go and see for herself. Disguising herself as a merchant, she took a few loads of wool to sell and set out to follow her husband.

Some days later, she arrived at the inn where he was living as a servant. They

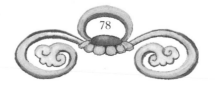

were very happy to see one another, and the young man told her everything that had happened. She told him to say nothing to the innkeeper and went inside and took a room for the night. As he usually did with his guests, the innkeeper invited her to dinner, and during dinner he managed to make the same bet with her as he'd made with her husband. If a cat came in with a lantern when night fell the next evening, the innkeeper was to have all her possessions, and if not, she was to have all of his.

The following day, the wife gave her husband a little box with three mice in it and some special instructions. Then she went to sit with the innkeeper to wait for the cat. Just at twilight, the big white cat started across the courtyard with the lantern in its mouth. The husband did what his wife had told him. He let out one of the mice, which ran right in front of the cat. The cat jumped in the air and almost ran after the mouse. But it had been so well trained, it regained control of itself and continued across the courtyard with the lantern. The husband let out another mouse, which also scampered right in front of the cat. The cat was so tempted that it stopped and turned around in a circle three times, but still its training held, and it continued towards the doorway with the lantern. When it was just about to open the door, the husband released the last mouse. This time the temptation was too much for the cat. It dropped the lantern and ran off after the mouse.

Darkness fell and the cat never appeared with the lantern. The innkeeper finally had to admit that he had lost his bet. He handed over to the disguised wife not only his own property but also everything he had won from her husband. The young man and his wife, taking all these possessions with them, returned to their own house, and they lived happily ever after.

SOURCES

"The Living Kuan Yin": Carol Kendal and Yao-wen Li, *Sweet and Sour* (Seabury Press, New York, 1978).

"The Most Important Thing": Seikan Hasegawa, *The Cave of Poison Grass* (Great Ocean Publishers, Arlington, VA, 1975).

"The Man Who Didn't Want to Die": Yei Theodora Ozaki, *Japanese Fairy Book* (Charles E. Tuttle Company, Tokyo, 1970).

"Useless Work": oral tradition.

"The Conch Maiden" and **"Goodheart and the Goddess of the Forest"**: D. and M Stovickova, *Tibetische Märchen: Märchen, Mythen und Legenden aus Tibet und anderen Ländern des Ferne Ostens* (Verlag Werner Dausien, Hanau, 1974).

"The Wisdom of the Crows": Post Wheeler, *Tales from the Japanese Storytellers* (Charles E. Tuttle Company, Tokyo, 1964).

"The Stone Ape": Lim Sian-tek, *Folk Tales from China* (John Day Company, New York, 1944).

"Where Are You Going?", **"Learning to be Silent"** and **"The Death of a Teacup"**: Paul Reps, *Zen Flesh, Zen Bones* (Anchor Books, Doubleday & Company, Garden City, NY, no date).

"Angulimala the Brigand": Sherab Chödzin Kohn, *The Awakened One* (Shambhala Publications, Boston, 1994).

"The Foolish Boy": Captain W. F. O'Connor, *Folk-Tales from Tibet* (Hurst and Blackett, London, 1906).

The tales gathered in this collection are all traditional ones and may also have appeared elsewhere than in the sources given above.

Text copyright © 1997 by Sherab Chödzin and Alexandra Kohn. Illustrations copyright © 1997 by Marie Cameron. First published in Great Britain in 1997 by Barefoot Books Ltd. Graphic Design: Design/Section. All rights reserved. No part of this book may be reproduced in any form without the written permission of the publisher, except in the case of brief quotations embodied in critical articles or reviews. Tricycle Press, P.O. Box 7123, Berkeley, California 94707.

Library of Congress Cataloging-in-Publication Data. Chödzin, Sherab. [Barefoot book of Buddhist tales] The wisdom of the crows and other Buddhist tales / retold by Sherab Chödzin & Alexandra Kohn ; illustrated by Marie Cameron. p. cm. Originally published: The barefoot book of Buddhist tales. England: Barefoot Books, 1997. Includes bibliographical references (p. 80). Summary: A collection of thirteen retold Buddhist tales from all over Asia, illustrating various aspects of Buddhist thought. ISBN 1-883672-68-6 (alk. paper) 1. Buddhist stories, English. [1. Buddhist stories.] I. Kohn, Alexandra. II. Cameron, Marie, ill. III. Title. BQ5810.C56 1998 294.3'8—dc21 97-30441 CIP AC

First Tricycle Press printing, 1998. Printed in Hong Kong
1 2 3 4 5 6 — 02 01 00 99 98

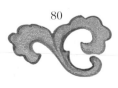